Grasslands Experiments

11 Science Experiments in One Hour or Less

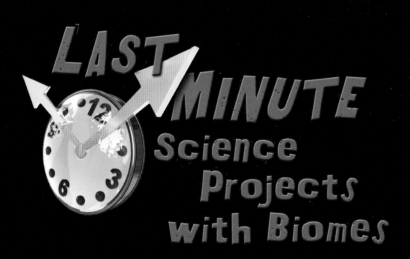

Last Minute Science Projects with Biomes

ROBERT GARDNER

ILLUSTRATED BY TOM LABAFF

Enslow Publishers, Inc.
40 Industrial Road
Box 398
Berkeley Heights, NJ 07922
USA

http://www.enslow.com

Library of Congress Cataloging-in-Publication Data

Gardner, Robert, 1929-

Grasslands experiments : 11 science experiments in one hour or less / Robert Gardner.

p. cm. — (Last minute science projects with biomes)

Summary: "A variety of science projects related to the grasslands that can be done in under an hour, plus a few that take longer for interested students"— Provided by publisher.

Includes index.

ISBN 978-0-7660-5927-6

1. Grassland ecology—Experiments—Juvenile literature. 2. Grasslands—Experiments—Juvenile literature. 3. Science projects—Juvenile literature. I. Title.

QH541.5.P7G7125 2015

577.4′078—dc23

2013008784

Future editions:

Paperback ISBN 978-0-7660-5928-3

ePUB ISBN 978-0-7660-5929-0

Single-User PDF ISBN 978-0-7660-5930-6

Multi-User PDF ISBN 978-0-7660-5931-3

Printed in the United States of America

052014 Lake Book Manufacturing, Inc., Melrose Park, IL

10 9 8 7 6 5 4 3 2 1

To Our Readers: We have done our best to make sure all Internet Addresses in this book were active and appropriate when we went to press. However, the author and the publisher have no control over and assume no liability for the material available on those Internet sites or on other Web sites they may link to. Any comments or suggestions can be sent by e-mail to comments@enslow.com or to the address on the back cover.

♻ Enslow Publishers, Inc., is committed to printing our books on recycled paper. The paper in every book contains 10% to 30% post-consumer waste (PCW). The cover board on the outside of each book contains 100% PCW. Our goal is to do our part to help young people and the environment too!

Photo Credits: ©1999 Artville, LLC, p. 13; Dorling KindersleyRF/©Thinkstock, p. 33; Library of Congress Prints and Photographs, p. 19; National Archives, p. 27; Shutterstock.com: ©dvande, p. 5, ©Tom Reichner, p. 6, ©StockLite, p. 7, ©JLR Photography, p. 16, ©Dan Howell, p. 25, ©Tish 1, p. 39

Illustration Credits: Tom Labaff (tomlabaff.com)

Cover Credits: Shutterstock.com: © Djomas(main figure), ©Onur YILDIRIM (clock with yellow arrows), ©Bayanova Svetlana, (grass), ©Lim Yong Hian(stained glass flower), nbriam(blue table fan); volk65/iStock/©Thinkstock, (blue and yellow pinwheel).

Contents

Last Minute Science Projects with Biomes

Are You Running Late?   4
Grassland Biomes   4
The Scientific Method   8
Science Fairs   9
Safety First   10
A Note About Your Notebook   11

30 Minutes or Less   12
1   Using Maps (20 minutes)   12
2   A Climatogram of a City (20 minutes)   14
3   Grassland and Compacted Soil (20 minutes)   16
4   Reducing Wind Erosion (20 minutes)   18
5   Seasons in a Grassland (30 minutes)   20
6   The Drying Effect of Prairie Wind (30 minutes)   22
7   Cowboy Hats on the Prairie (30 minutes)   24

One Hour or Less   26
8   Settling America's Prairie: The Homestead Act and Arithmetic (1 hour)   26
9   How Much of an Aquifer Is Water? (1 hour)   28
10 A Model Wind Turbine (1 hour)   30

11 Global Warming and the Greenhouse Effect (1 hour)   32

One Month or Less   36
12 Grassland Soil and the Dust Bowl (1 day)   36
13 A Model Aquifer and Drought (several days)   38
14 Seeds in Different "Biomes" (several days)   42
15 How Does Your Rainfall Compare With Grassland Rainfall? (1 month or more)   44

Words to Know   46

Learn More (Books and Websites)   47

Index   48

🎗 Contains ideas for science fair projects.

Are You Running Late?

Do you have a science project that is due soon, maybe tomorrow? Then this book is for you! It is filled with experiments about grassland biomes. Most of the experiments can be done in less than one hour. An estimate of the time needed is given for each experiment. But perhaps you have plenty of time to prepare for your next science project or science fair. You can still use and enjoy this book.

Many experiments are followed by a "Keep Exploring" section. There you will find ideas for more science projects. The details are left to you, the young scientist. You can design and carry out your own experiments, under adult supervision, when you have more time.

For some experiments, you may need a partner to help you. Work with someone who likes to do experiments as much as you do. Then you will both enjoy what you are doing. In this book, if any safety issue or danger is involved in doing an experiment, you will be warned. In some cases you will be asked to work with an adult. Please do so. Don't take any chances that could lead to an injury.

Grassland Biomes

A biome is a region of the earth with a particular climate. The plants and animals that live in a biome are quite similar all around the world. This book is about grassland biomes. But there are other biomes. Earth's land biomes include deserts, tundra, taiga, grasslands, rain forests, and temperate forests.

There are 10,000 different species, or types, of natural grass. There are also grasses that are grown to feed humans and other animals. Grasses grown for food include wheat, oats, barley, corn, and rice.

Temperate grasslands get between 10 and 30 inches of rain a year. This is more rain than a desert but less than a temperate forest. Tropical grasslands, or savannas, are warmer grasslands. They need more water. They require 24 to 59 inches of rain each year.

In the United States, there are grasslands (prairies) from the Mississippi River to the Rocky Mountains and south from central Canada to the Gulf of Mexico. Moving west, the prairie grass gradually shortens. It starts at three to ten feet and becomes as short as five to twelve inches near the Rockies. When the soil is deep and rich, and rainfall is plentiful, the grass grows taller. The eastern tall grass grows on deep, rich soil that receives 24 to 30 inches of rain each year. The short grass growing on the semiarid, shallow western soil receives only 10 to 16 inches of rain per year.

Before white settlers turned much of the prairie into farms and ranches, Native Americans roamed the biome. Bison grazed on the prairie grass. The animals provided these people with most of their needs. Bison skins clothed their bodies and covered their tepees. The bison

Bison are a native grassland animal.

provided meat for nourishment. Bison bones were used to make tools. Wood was scarce on the grassland. Dried bison dung was gathered and used as fuel for fires.

During the 1800s, white hunters killed most of the bison, but a few small herds still remain. Today, cattle and sheep are the main grazers on this grassland. The major wild predator is the coyote. Coyotes have replaced wolves. Until recently, wolves had been hunted to near extinction. Other animals that can be found on the prairie include jackrabbits, prairie dogs, ground squirrels, pronghorn antelope, mule deer, rattlesnakes, a variety of birds, and other animals.

During the 1920s, tractors were used to plow the prairie sod. Much of the buffalo grass, grama grass, bluestem, and other grasses were replaced with wheat, corn, cotton, and oilseed crops such as canola and sunflower.

Prairie dogs live in grasslands.

This field of canola is in bloom with yellow flowers. Canola grass is an important crop. Canola oil is made from canola seeds.

In the 1930s, a long drought dried the soil that farmers had plowed. Strong winds, a common feature of North American grasslands, lifted the soil and carried it in thick clouds of dust. The dust clouds blew eastward across the country. The western dust could even be detected by ships on the Atlantic Ocean. A large section of the grasslands became known as the dust bowl. Many farmers whose soil was blown away abandoned their farms and moved to California.

Grasslands can be found all around the world. Grasslands have different names in other continents. What we call grassland or prairie is known as steppes in Eurasia and Asia, pampas in Argentina, and veldt in South Africa.

The Scientific Method

To do experiments the way scientists do, you need to know about the scientific method. It is true that scientists in different areas of science use different ways of experimenting. Depending on the problem, one method is likely to be better than another.

Despite these differences, all scientists use a similar approach as they experiment. It is called the scientific method. In most experimenting, some or all of the following steps are used: making an observation, coming up with a question, creating a hypothesis (a possible answer to the question) and a prediction (an if-then statement), designing and conducting an experiment, analyzing results, drawing conclusions about the prediction, and deciding if the hypothesis is true or false. Scientists share the results of their experiments by writing articles that are published in science journals.

You might wonder, How do I use the scientific method? You begin when you see, read, or hear about something in the world that makes you curious. So you ask a question. To find an answer, you do a well-designed investigation; you use the scientific method.

Once you have a question, you can make a hypothesis. Your hypothesis is a possible answer to the question (what you think is true). For example, you might hypothesize that rainfall in a grassland is less than it is in a temperate forest. Once you have a hypothesis, it is time to design an experiment to test your hypothesis.

In most cases, you should do a controlled experiment. This means having two subjects that are treated the same except for the one thing being tested. That thing is called a variable. For example, to test the hypothesis above, you might measure the annual rainfall in a grassland and in a temperate forest over a decade. If you found that the rainfall in the grassland was significantly less than in the forest, you might conclude that your hypothesis was correct.

The results of one experiment often lead to another question. In the case above, that experiment might lead you to ask, What effect does less rainfall have on the kind of plants and animals found in a grassland? Whatever the results, something can be learned from every experiment!

Science Fairs

Some of the investigations in this book contain ideas that might be used as a science fair project. Those ideas are indicated with a symbol (🎖) on the Contents page. However, judges at science fairs do not reward projects or experiments that are copied from a book. For example, a diagram of a leaf would not impress most judges. An experiment that measures the effect of rainfall on the growth rate of grass would be more likely to interest them.

Science fair judges tend to reward creative thought and imagination. It is difficult to be creative or imaginative unless you are really interested in your project. Therefore, try to choose something that excites you. And before you jump into a project, consider your own talents. Consider too the cost of the materials you will need.

If you decide to use an experiment or idea found in this book as a science fair project, find ways to modify or extend it. This should not be difficult. As you carry out investigations, new ideas will come to mind. You will think of questions that experiments can answer. The experiments will make excellent science fair projects This is especially true when the ideas are yours and are interesting to you.

Safety First

Safety is very important in science. Some of the rules below may seem obvious to you, others may not, but it is important that you follow all of them.

1. Do any experiments or projects **under the adult supervision** of a science teacher or knowledgeable adult.

2. Read all instructions carefully before proceeding with a project. If you have questions, check with your supervisor before going further.

3. **Always wear safety goggles** when doing experiments that could cause particles to enter your eyes. Tie back long hair and do not wear open-toed shoes.

4. Do not eat or drink while experimenting. Never taste substances being used (unless instructed to do so).

5. Do not touch chemicals.

6. Do not let water drops fall on a hot lightbulb.

7. The liquid in some older thermometers is mercury (a dense liquid metal). It is dangerous to touch mercury or breathe its vapor. That is why mercury thermometers have been banned in many states. When doing experiments, use only non-mercury thermometers, such as digital thermometers or those filled with alcohol. If you have a mercury thermometer in the house, **ask an adult** to take it to a place where it can be exchanged or safely discarded.

8. Do only those experiments that are described in the book or those that have been approved by an adult.

9. Maintain a serious attitude while conducting experiments. Never engage in horseplay or practical jokes.

10. Remove all items not needed for the experiment from your work space.

11. At the end of every activity, clean all materials used and put them away. Then wash your hands thoroughly with soap and water.

A Note About Your Notebook

Your notebook, as any scientist will tell you, is a valuable possession. It should contain ideas you may have as you experiment, sketches you draw, calculations you make, and hypotheses you suggest. It should include a description of every experiment you do and the data you record, such as volumes, temperatures, masses, and so on. It should also contain the results of your experiments, graphs you draw, and any conclusions you make based on your results.

30 Minutes or Less

Here are experiments about grassland biomes. You can do them in 30 minutes or less. If you need a science project by tomorrow, not much time is left, so let's get started!

1 Using Maps (20 minutes)

What's the Plan?

Let's find out where grassland biomes are located around the world. And let's find out in which type of biome you live.

WHAT YOU NEED:

- **map of biomes in Figure 1**

- **map of the world or large world globe**

What You Do

1. Examine the map in Figure 1. It shows where grassland and other biomes are located.

2. Look at the places where grassland biomes are found. Compare them with the same places on a map of the world or on a world globe.

3. On which continents do grasslands exist? Are there any continents that do not have a grassland biome?

4. Find where you live on a world map. Using Figure 1, find the biome where you live.

What's Going On?

You compared the map of biomes in Figure 1 with a map of the world. You could see that grasslands, either temperate or tropical, are found on every continent except Antarctica.

By a similar comparison, you could see in which type of biome you live. Don't be surprised if you think the map of biomes for your home is wrong. The map shows what is true for much of the region where you live, not every part of it. For example, the author lives on Cape Cod in Massachusetts. The biome map indicates that he lives in a temperate forest biome. However, the outer end of Cape Cod is covered by sand dunes. Also, while forest covers much of Cape Cod, the trees are shorter than in a typical temperate forest. This is caused by the strong winds and salt air coming off the Atlantic Ocean.

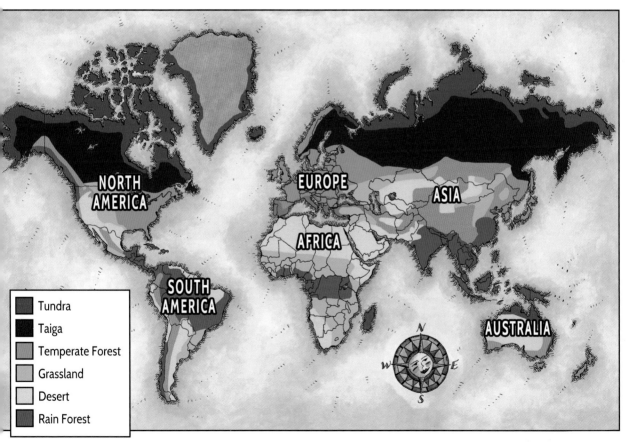

Figure 1. You can see the six land biomes of the world. What biome do you live in?

2 A Climatogram of a City (20 minutes)

What's the Plan?

Let's make a climatogram for Canton, South Dakota.

WHAT YOU NEED:
- graph paper
- pen or pencil
- Table 1

What You Do

1. Figure 2 shows what a climatogram looks like. Months of the year are plotted along the horizontal axis. Rainfall is shown along the left vertical axis, temperature along the right vertical axis.

2. Use a sheet of graph paper to make a climatogram for Canton, South Dakota. The climatogram will show Canton's average monthly temperature and rainfall. The data in Table 1 provides the information you need to make a climatogram for Canton, South Dakota.

Table 1: Monthly average temperatures and rainfall for Canton, SD.												
	Jan	Feb	Mar	Apr	May	Jun	Jul	Aug	Sept	Oct	Nov	Dec
Temp (°C)	–9.4	–5.8	1.1	9.2	15.8	21.0	23.6	22.0	16.8	10.2	1.2	–6.9
Rainfall (in)	0.4	0.7	1.5	2.3	3.0	4.0	2.9	3.5	2.9	1.5	1.0	0.7

3. What is the approximate average temperature for one year in Canton?

4. What is the approximate total average rainfall for one year in Canton?

5. Are Canton's temperatures and rainfall normal for a grassland biome? Does Canton have warm summers and cold winters? Does it have 10 to 30 inches of rain?

What's Going On?

Your climatogram should show Canton's average monthly temperature and rainfall in a graphical way. The approximate total rainfall in Canton is 24.4 inches. The approximate average annual temperature is 8.2°C (46.8°F). These numbers are normal for a grassland biome.

Keep Exploring—If You Have More Time!

• Prepare a climatogram of your city or town. What is your total yearly rainfall? Do you have cold winters and warm summers? What is your average annual temperature?

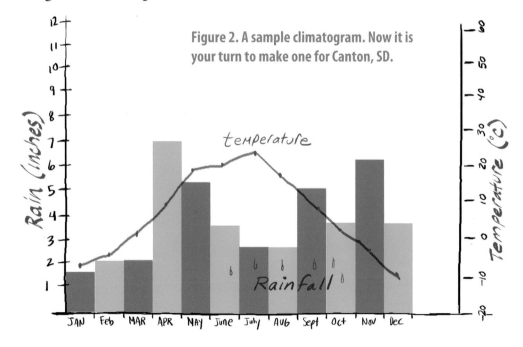

Figure 2. A sample climatogram. Now it is your turn to make one for Canton, SD.

3 Grassland and Compacted Soil (20 minutes)

What's the Plan?

Ranchers use the grasslands as pasture for their cattle. These hoofed grazing animals may compact (press together) the soil by repeatedly walking on it. The wheels of heavy machinery, such as tractors, may also compact the soil. Let's see if compacted soil acts differently from regular loose soil.

WHAT YOU NEED:

- **2 small containers, such as 6-ounce plastic yogurt cups or paper cups**
- **garden soil**
- **gloves**
- **medicine cup or vial**
- **water**

Cattle graze on a grassland.

16

What You Do

1. Find two small containers, such as 6-ounce plastic yogurt cups or paper cups. Nearly fill the cups with garden soil.

2. Put on gloves. Use your fingers to thoroughly compact (press together) the soil in one cup. Leave the soil loose in the other cup.

3. Fill a medicine cup or vial with water. Pour the water onto the compacted soil. Pour an equal amount of water onto the loose soil. What do you observe? What is the effect of compacted soil on percolation (the movement of water into soil)? What might be the effect of compacted soil on erosion? On plant growth?

4. Empty the soil in a garden. Discard the containers, and wash your hands thoroughly.

What's Going On?

When soil is compacted, it is more difficult for water and air to enter the soil and reach the roots of plants. It is also difficult for roots to push through the soil as they grow. Roots absorb most of a plant's water. The root cells need the oxygen in air. When rain or irrigation water falls on compacted soil, it is similar to water falling on pavement. Much of the water runs off and carries soil particles with it, causing soil erosion.

Leaving compacted land fallow (without crops or grazing animals) can often restore overgrazed land. The U.S. government used this simple method to restore some overgrazed federal rangeland.

4 Reducing Wind Erosion (20 minutes)

What's the Plan?

Grassland farmers often plant trees or bushes to create hedgerows around their crop fields. Let's see why they do this.

What You Do

1. In a basement, a garage, or outdoors, prepare a cardboard box and a pile of dry sand as shown in Figure 3. Put the box and sand on a small table, the floor, or the ground.

2. Put on safety glasses. Use a hair dryer or small fan to create a wind that blows on the sand. What happens?

3. Replace the sand and repeat the experiment. But this time, let a piece of cardboard represent a hedgerow. Hold the cardboard between the hair dryer and the sand.

4. Turn on the hair dryer or fan to create a wind. Let the wind blow on the hedgerow for several minutes. How does the hedgerow reduce wind erosion?

WHAT YOU NEED:

- **cardboard box**
- **dry sand**
- **small table (optional)**
- **safety glasses**
- **hair dryer or small fan**
- **electrical outlet**
- **piece of cardboard**

Figure 3. How does wind cause soil erosion?

18

What's Going On?

The hedgerow blocks or reduces the wind. As a result, less soil is blown away.

The Great Dust Storm

During the 1920s, tractors plowed the prairie grasslands in order to plant wheat. United States wheat production doubled in less than ten years. During a long drought, the prairie soil became dry. In 1934, a windstorm created a dust cloud three miles high. It covered more than a million square miles. It stretched from Canada to Texas and from Montana to Ohio. Prairie dust fell on ships 300 miles east of the U.S. Atlantic coast. And more dust storms followed. Three hundred blew across North Dakota during an eight-month period. Oklahoma suffered through 102 such storms in a single year.

Keep Exploring–If You Have More Time!

* Design and do experiments to see which type or types of dry and wet soil are most resistant to wind erosion. You might try sand, garden soil, potting soil, and clay soil.

Dust storms in the 1930s blew clouds of dry grassland soil.

5 Seasons in a Grassland (30 minutes)

What's the Plan?

Let's do an experiment to see why grasslands in the United States have seasons.

WHAT YOU NEED:
- **sheet of paper**
- **table**
- **dark room**
- **large protractor**
- **flashlight**

What You Do

Grasslands have warm summers and cold winters. The U.S. grasslands along a latitude of 40 degrees stretch across the states of Utah, Colorado, the Kansas–Nebraska border, and on across Missouri and Illinois. At the beginning of summer (June 21), the midday sun at this latitude reaches an altitude of 73.5 degrees. At the beginning of winter (December 21), the midday sun is only 26.5 degrees above the horizon.

1. Place a sheet of paper on a table. Turn off lights or close shades to make the room dark.

2. Hold a large protractor upright on the paper.

3. Let a flashlight represent the sun. Shine the light onto the paper at an angle of about 73 degrees (Figure 4a). Notice the light on the paper. The paper represents grassland at 40 degrees latitude.

4. Move the flashlight so that it strikes the paper at an angle of about 26 degrees (Figure 4b). Again, notice the light that shines on the paper.

What's Going On?

As you saw, the winter light on the grasslands is not as intense as the summer light. The winter sunlight is more spread out. The same amount of light, at

20

26 degrees, covers a larger area, making the winter light less intense. The more direct summer sunlight provides greater warmth to the biome. During winter, the less intense light causes air temperatures to fall. The result of the sun's different angles help explain grassland seasons. Also, the winter sun passes through more atmosphere where some of its energy is absorbed.

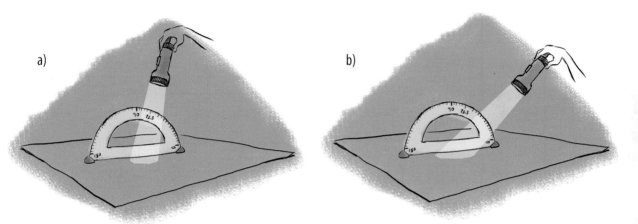

Figure 4. a) The sun at midday on June 21 is 73.5 degrees above the horizon at a latitude of 40 degrees. The sun's intense light warms U.S. grasslands as this model shows. b) The winter sunlight has a longer path through Earth's atmosphere. As a result, more of its energy is absorbed by the air.

Keep Exploring–If You Have More Time!

- Design and do an experiment to measure the altitude of the midday sun at the latitude where you live. Repeat the experiment at the beginning of each season.

- Midday is seldom at noon (12 p.m.). Do an experiment to find midday. Do it at different times of the year. Does it always occur at the same time?

6 The Drying Effect of Prairie Wind (30 minutes)

What's the Plan?

Let's find out how a prairie wind affects the evaporation of water.

What You Do

1. Add water to two identical folded paper towels.

2. Hold each towel, in turn, over a sink. Open each towel. Let any excess water in the towel drain into the sink.

3. Weigh each folded wet towel on a balance. Record the mass of each towel.

4. Open one towel. Use clothespins to hang the towel on a line in air that is not moving.

5. Open the second towel. Hang it on a line near a fan (Figure 5). Then turn on the fan.

6. After 20 minutes, reweigh both towels. Record the mass of each towel. From which towel did more water evaporate?

WHAT YOU NEED:

- water
- 2 identical paper towels
- a sink
- a balance
- pen or pencil
- notebook
- clothespins
- clothesline or heavy string
- a fan
- electrical outlet
- clock or watch

What's Going On?

You probably found that the towel in the fan's wind lost more mass than the towel that hung in still air. The experiment shows that the winds that often blow over America's prairies tend to dry the grasslands.

Keep Exploring–If You Have More Time!

* Design and do an experiment to compare the drying effect of wind on grass-covered soil versus damp garden soil.

* Do an experiment to see how wind speed affects the rate at which water evaporates.

Figure 5. How does wind affect the rate at which water evaporates?

7 Cowboy Hats on the Prairie (30 minutes)

What's the Plan?

Starting in the 1800s, cowboys worked on grassland ranches. They rode horses as they cared for the cattle and drove them to market. During summer months, it can be very warm and sunny on the prairie. You know that is true if you made the climatogram in Experiment 2. Many of the cowboys wore, and still wear, wide-brimmed Stetson hats sometimes called "ten-gallon hats." Let's see why they might have worn such hats.

WHAT YOU NEED:

- **2 thermometers (–10–50°C, or –20–120°F)**
- **bright sunlight**
- **large hat or a piece of cardboard**
- **clock or watch**
- **notebook**
- **pen or pencil**

What You Do

1. Place one thermometer in bright sunlight, as shown in Figure 6. Place a second thermometer nearby in shade created by a hat. If hat shade is not available, use a piece of cardboard to shade the second thermometer. (If you have only one thermometer, leave it in shade for 20 minutes. Then put it in the sun for the same amount of time.)

2. After about 20 minutes, read and record the temperature on both thermometers. What can you conclude?

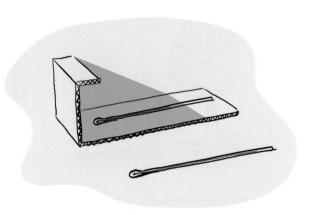

Figure 6. How do sun and shade affect temperature?

24

What's Going On?

The wide-brimmed, ten-gallon Stetson allowed cowboys to carry their shade from the sun with them. On the prairie, where trees were rare, shade from the hot sun was hard to find. The big hat sometimes provided the only shade they had. Shade, as you saw in your experiment, is a cooler place to be than the bright sun. Of course, Stetson's name for the hat—"The Boss of the Plains"—was probably a factor too.

Keep Exploring–If You Have More Time!

- Do an experiment to show that a smart cowboy would wear a white hat.

- Do an experiment to show that solar energy can be changed to electrical energy.

- Build a model to show how solar energy can be used to heat water.

A ten-gallon hat kept cowboys in the shade!

Only an hour left to prepare a science project? Here are experiments that meet your need.

8 Settling America's Prairie: The Homestead Act and Arithmetic (1 hour)

What's the Plan?

In 1862, Congress passed the Homestead Act. The act allowed the government to give a person 160 acres of grassland if he or she settled on the land and developed it. Let's get an idea of what 160 acres looks like.

> **WHAT YOU NEED:**
> - **football field**
> - **calculator**
> - **pedometer (optional)**
> - **long measuring tape**

What You Do

An acre is 43,560 square feet (ft^2). To give you an idea of what an acre looks like, go to a football field.

1. Stand on the ten-yard line. The distance to the opposite goal line times the width of the field is an area of approximately one acre.

2. Try to imagine 160 times that area. That area was the land given to a settler by the Homestead Act. Using a calculator, calculate the number of square feet in 160 acres.

3. The government land was divided into square lots. What is the length of a 160-acre lot?

4. If you have a pedometer and a long measuring tape, find the distance you go with each step. Then walk the length of a square 160-acre lot. How many of your steps equal the length of a square 160-acre lot?

5. How long and how wide is a 160-acre lot in miles?

What's Going On?

The area of 160 acres is: 160 x 43,560 ft^2 = 6,969,600 ft^2 or 0.25 mi^2.
The length of this square lot of land would be the square root of 6,969,600 ft^2.
That length is 2,640 feet or half a mile. Remember a mile is 5,280 feet.

Keep Exploring–If You Have More Time!

• How large is your school ground in square feet? In acres? in hectares?

This homesteading family sets out to settle in the grasslands of the United States.

9 How Much of an Aquifer Is Water? (1 hour)

What's the Plan?

A supply of water is found in the Ogallala Aquifer under U.S. grassland. An aquifer is underground water that fills the spaces between soil particles. The Ogallala Aquifer lies under much of our grasslands. It was formed by melting glaciers millions of years ago. Let's find out what fraction of an aquifer is water and what fraction is soil. We'll use sand to represent all the soil particles. The particles in soil are clay silt, gravel, and stones as well as sand.

WHAT YOU NEED:

- dry sand
- graduated cylinder or metric measuring cup
- pen or pencil
- notebook
- plastic or foam cup
- water

What You Do

1. Pour some dry sand into a graduated cylinder or metric measuring cup. Add sand until the cylinder or cup is about two-thirds full. Record the volume of the sand.

2. Pour the dry sand into a plastic or foam cup.

3. Pour water into the graduated cylinder or metric measuring cup. Add the water until it is about one-third full. Record the volume of the water.

4. Slowly pour the sand from the cup into the water in the graduated cylinder or measuring cup. The water will displace the air as it fills the spaces between the sand particles. Record the new volume—the volume of the sand and water.

5. What fraction of the sand was occupied by air and now by water? What percentage of an aquifer is water?

What's Going On?

Suppose the volume of dry sand was 70 cm^3 (70 mL). If the dry sand was added to 33 cm^3 of water, assume the total volume became 75 cm^3. The volume of the dry sand grains alone must have been the volume of sand and water together minus the volume of water alone. Therefore, the volume of sand grains was 42 cm^3 because: 75 cm^3 − 33 cm^3 = 42 cm^3.

The volume of air in the sand equals the volume of dry sand with air minus the volume of sand without air. Therefore, the volume of air in the sand is 70 cm^3 − 42 cm^3 = 28 cm^3.

Now those spaces are filled with water. Therefore, the percentage of the space occupied by water, previously air, is 40 percent because: 28 cm^3/70 cm^3 = 0.40 = 40%.

10 A Model Wind Turbine (1 hour)

What's the Plan?

The U.S. prairie is a windy place. The wind can be used to generate electricity. Let's make a miniature model wind turbine that can generate electricity.

What You Do

A toy electric motor has one or more coils of wire that can turn between magnets. When the coils turn, the magnetic field through the coils will change. Electric charges will be pushed along the wires. The motor becomes an electric generator.

1. Examine a small electric motor. There should be two small metal leads outside the metal case. These leads are connected to the motor's coils. Use two insulated wires with alligator clips to connect the motor's two leads to the poles of a milliammeter or a microammeter. (A milliammeter measures thousandths of an ampere. A microammeter measures millionths of an ampere.) Electric currents (moving charges) are measured in units called amperes.

2. Spin the motor's shaft with your fingers. The meter will show that an electric current is being generated.

3. To model the propellers of a wind turbine, you can use a pinwheel. Pinwheels differ, so you will have to figure out a way to connect the pinwheel to the generator (motor) shaft. **With help from an adult**, you may be able to use a wood dowel, rubber or plastic tubing, and tape to make the connection. One example is shown in Figure 7a.

4. Use wires with alligator clips to connect the generator to a milliammeter or a microammeter. Wind from a fast-spinning fan can turn the pinwheel turbine (Figure 7b). Does the generator produce an electric current when turned by the wind?

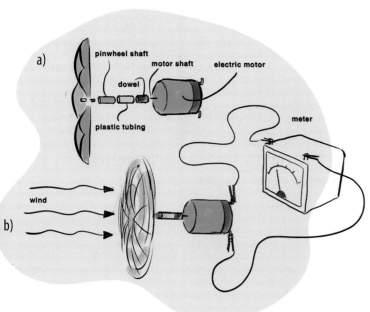

Figure 7. a) A drilled wood dowel may fit onto the motor shaft. An adult can drill a hole in the dowel to fit the shaft. Plastic or rubber tubing may also work here. Or both tubing and dowel can be used. b) Connect the motor to a milliammeter or a microammeter. Use outdoor wind or wind from a fan to turn the pinwheel turbine.

What's Going On?

Wind turns the pinwheel. The pinwheel is connected to the generator (toy motor) so the motor shaft turns. The shaft turns the motor's coils, which are in a magnetic field. This causes the electric current that is indicated by the meter.

11 Global Warming and the Greenhouse Effect (1 hour)

What's the Plan?

The sun shines constantly on the earth. Fortunately, some of that solar energy is radiated back into space. If Earth did not send some of the energy it receives back into space, our planet would be too hot for life. However, if all the sun's energy we receive were reradiated into space, Earth would be frozen. Earth's atmosphere acts as an insulating blanket. It protects us from extreme temperatures. During daylight hours, the atmosphere absorbs and reradiates about half the sun's energy back to outer space. At night, carbon dioxide, water vapor, and other gases in the atmosphere absorb some of the energy being radiated by the warm earth. These gases, called greenhouse gases, radiate some of the energy they absorb back to Earth.

> **WHAT YOU NEED:**
> - **2 identical thermometers**
> - **clear plastic container that can be tightly closed**
> - **a few green leaves**
> - **bright sunlight**
> - **automobile**
> - **clock or watch**

A greenhouse behaves in a similar manner. The glass covering a greenhouse lets in all wavelengths of visible sunlight. The plants, soil, and other matter within the greenhouse absorb much of this radiation. But they reradiate much of the energy they absorb as invisible infrared light. Infrared light has longer wavelengths and less energy than visible light. But glass will not let infrared radiation through. As a result, the energy in infrared light, which we sense as heat, is reflected back into the greenhouse. Much of the solar energy that entered the greenhouse as visible light cannot escape once it is reradiated with longer

The greenhouse effect: The sun's energy (yellow) enters Earth's atmosphere. Some of that energy (orange) is reradiated back to space. Other energy (red) is sent back to Earth's surface.

wavelengths. As a result, the heat and temperature within the greenhouse increase.

Earth acts like a giant greenhouse. Its window is atmospheric carbon dioxide (CO_2) and other greenhouse gases. Atmospheric carbon dioxide has been increasing as we burn more and more fossil fuels (coal and oil). As more carbon dioxide enters the atmosphere, more heat is reradiated back to Earth. Some scientists estimate that the earth's average temperature will rise by 3°C (5°F) during this century. This global warming is already melting arctic glaciers. The melted water flows into the ocean. The added water is causing a rise in sea level that will flood many coastal areas.

Other effects of global warming include increasingly severe storms, droughts, and forest fires. These weather events have already struck America's grasslands and forests. As global temperatures continue to rise, we may well experience weather that may become even more severe.

Let's build a small model greenhouse. The model will show you how the greenhouse effect works.

What You Do

1. Obtain two identical thermometers.

2. Put one thermometer in a clear plastic container that can be tightly closed. Add a few green leaves to represent plants. This container will be the "greenhouse."

3. Put the "greenhouse" in bright sunlight. Put the second thermometer beside the "greenhouse" (Figure 8).

4. Watch both thermometers for a few minutes. What do you observe?

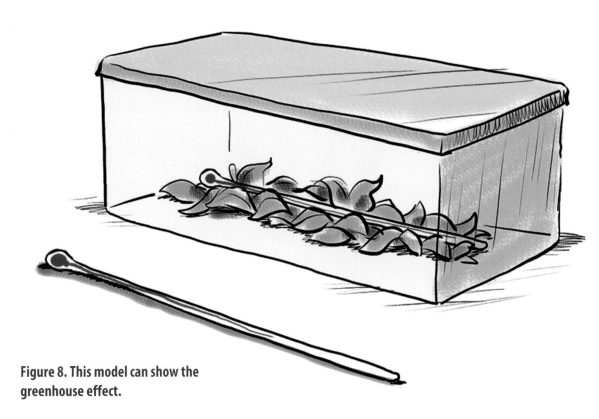

Figure 8. This model can show the greenhouse effect.

34

5. Place a thermometer in a car that is at rest in bright sunlight. Record the temperature. Close the windows of the car.

6. After 20 minutes, return to the car. What is the temperature now? What evidence do you have that a car is a greenhouse on wheels?

What's Going On?

The miniature greenhouse that you built behaved like a larger real greenhouse. It allowed sunlight's longer visible wavelengths of light to enter the box. But it "trapped" the energy inside, causing the temperature inside the box to become greater than the temperature outside. The car also behaved like a greenhouse. That is why you should never leave animals or young children in a closed automobile. The air inside can become very hot.

Keep Exploring–If You Have More Time!

• Add black construction paper to the bottom of a second "greenhouse" like the one you used in Experiment 11. Place the two greenhouses in bright sunlight. Predict which one will grow warmer faster. Explain your results.

One Month or Less

1 month or less

Here are experiments that require more time. However, if you are a budding scientist, it will be time well spent!

12 Grassland Soil and the Dust Bowl (1 day)

What's the Plan?

A long, severe drought in the 1930s led to dust storms that carried away grassland soil. Let's do an experiment to see why winds carried the soil away. Let's see, too, why not plowing the soil could have saved it.

What You Do

1. Place a tablespoonful of fine garden soil on a piece of paper. Shine a strong lightbulb on the soil until it is thoroughly dry. This may take several hours. Crush any lumps of soil you have dried to make a fine, dry, powdery soil.

2. At the edge of a cardboard box, place the soil you have dried. Also place there a tablespoonful of moist garden soil and a small chunk of grass-covered soil.

3. Put the box outside. Let a strong wind blow across the soil samples. Or put the box and soil samples in a basement or garage. Use a fan or hair dryer to create a strong wind on the soils (Figure 9). What happens?

What's Going On?

You probably found that the wind blew some or all of the dry soil into the box. The grass-covered soil remained in place. Most of the damp soil probably also remained in place.

Plowing under grassland to plant wheat left no roots or stubble to hold the soil. When drought dried the soil, prairie winds blew much of it away. Many farmers, discouraged by drought and loss of soil, left their farms and moved to California.

Keep Exploring–If You Have More Time!

* Collect soil samples from different places. Can you find any living things in the soils?

* Dry the samples. Examine each sample with a powerful magnifier. What do you find in the soils? What do you conclude is the composition of the soils you examined?

Figure 9. You can test soil samples with wind.

13 A Model Aquifer and Drought (several days)

What's the Plan?

An aquifer is underground water that fills the spaces between soil particles. The Ogallala Aquifer lies under much of our grasslands. It was formed by melting glaciers millions of years ago. Today farmers and ranchers pump water from the Ogallala to irrigate their crops and water their cattle. Unfortunately, they remove more water from the aquifer than is returned by rain. Let's make a model aquifer. Then we'll see what happens when we pump too much water from it.

WHAT YOU NEED:

- clear aquarium, clear plastic shoe box, or a large clear bowl
- sand
- ruler
- water
- watering can
- large, clear plastic vial
- eyedropper
- green food coloring

What You Do

1. Use sand to cover the bottom of a clear aquarium, clear plastic shoe box, or a large clear bowl. Add sand until it is about 7 to 10 cm (3 to 4 in) deep. The glass or plastic bottom of the container can represent bedrock under the soil. Water can't go through bedrock.

2. Move the sand to form model hills and valleys. The lowest "valley" in the sand should be at least a centimeter (1/2 in) above the "bedrock."

3. Slowly sprinkle water from a watering can onto the sand. From the side, watch the "rain" sink into the soil.

4. Observe the formation of an "aquifer" (water filling the spaces between the sand). The top of the aquifer is called the water table.

5. Add more "rain." Watch the water table rise. Notice how "ponds" are created in the valleys as the water table rises.

6. Create a "drought." Add no more water for several days. Watch ponds dry up as the "water table" falls. Then add a little more "rain" and notice the rising level of the aquifer's water table.

Crop irrigation uses lots of underground water.

7. During the "drought," make a smaller model aquifer. Add dry sand to a large, clear plastic vial. Add sand until the vial is about three-quarters full.

8. Using an eyedropper, make it "rain" on the sand. Watch the water move down through the sand, creating an aquifer. Continue "raining" until a "pond" covers the aquifer as might happen during a flood.

9. Make a "well" in the aquifer (Figure 10). Push an eyedropper to the bottom of the vial at one side of the aquifer.

10. The eyedropper can also serve as a "pump." Use the pump to remove water from the aquifer. On the grassland biome, the water might be given to thirsty cattle or to irrigate crops. Pump out as much water as possible. What happens to an aquifer's water table if the water is pumped out faster than it is put back?

11. Sometimes an aquifer can become polluted by a harmful or poisonous chemical. To "pollute"

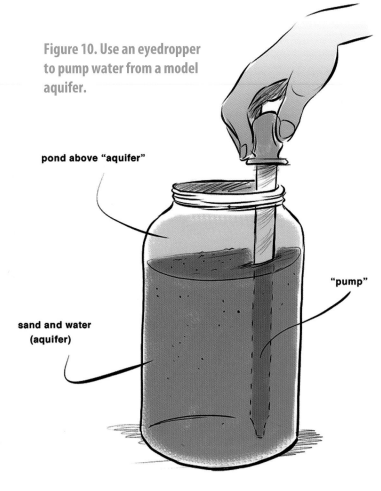

Figure 10. Use an eyedropper to pump water from a model aquifer.

pond above "aquifer"

"pump"

sand and water (aquifer)

the model aquifer, add a drop or two of green food coloring to the sand. The green food coloring represents pollution.

12. "Rain" clear water onto the sand again. What happens to the "pollution"?

13. Pump the aquifer again. Continue to rain on and pump the aquifer several times. Why does the well become polluted?

14. Do an experiment to see if the pollution can be removed by many rains and pumpings.

15. How might a polluted aquifer be cleaned up?

What's Going On?

As you have seen, gravity causes water to move downward into soil. The water fills the spaces that exist between particles of soil. If the water table is higher than low ground, a pond or lake will exist. If water is pumped out of the aquifer faster than it is replaced, the water table is lowered.

Pumping is lowering the Ogallala Aquifer's water table. As a result, deeper wells have to be drilled to reach the water. Then more powerful pumps have to bought to force the water up to the ground. Because grasslands receive only 10 to 30 inches of rain per year, prairie farmers and ranchers face a crisis. Similar problems with aquifers exist throughout the world. And a rising world population makes the problem even more serious.

Sometimes pollution can be reduced or removed from an aquifer by repeated pumpings.

14 Seeds in Different "Biomes" (several days)

What's the Plan?

Let's see how well seeds germinate (grow) in grassland and other biomes.

What You Do

1. Add some dry sand to a small aluminum pan. Bury several winter rye or radish seeds in the sand. Put this "desert biome" in a warm, dry place.

2. In another small aluminum pan add some garden soil. Bury several winter rye or radish seeds in the soil. Put this "tundra biome" in a cold place such as a refrigerator. Keep the soil damp, not wet.

3. Put some garden soil in another small aluminum pan. Then add some grass-covered soil. Bury several winter rye or radish seeds in the soil around the grass Put this "grassland biome" in a warm place. Keep the soil damp, not wet.

4. In another small aluminum pan add a damp piece of paper towel. Place several winter rye or radish seeds on the towel. Cover the seeds with another damp piece of paper towel. Then cover the pan and contents. A large jar cover will do nicely. The towels need to be kept damp, not wet. Put this "rain forest biome" in a warm place.

WHAT YOU NEED:

- **5 small aluminum pans**
- **dry sand**
- **winter rye or radish seeds**
- **warm, dry place**
- **garden soil**
- **refrigerator**
- **water**
- **grass—covered soil**
- **paper towels**
- **large jar cover**

5. Finally, put several rye or radish seeds in a small aluminum pan nearly filled with water. Cover the pan. Put it in a warm place. This pan might represent a pond in a forest biome.

What's Going On?

To germinate, seeds need water, oxygen, and a warm temperature. Seeds in the desert won't germinate unless it rains. Seeds in the tundra won't germinate until temperatures become warmer. Seeds in the warm, moist rain forest will germinate quickly. Seeds in the pond may begin to germinate. But they soon run out of oxygen and stop growing. There is not enough oxygen dissolved in water to allow germination to continue.

Keep Exploring–If You Have More Time!

- Soak some lima bean seeds overnight. Then carefully dissect the seeds to find the embryo plants.

15 How Does Your Rainfall Compare With Grassland Rainfall? (1 month or more)

What's the Plan?

To measure rainfall, you need a rain gauge. Then you can compare your rainfall with that found in a grassland town or city. If you don't have a rain gauge, you can make one.

What You'll Do

1. Pour water into a large jar until it is exactly one inch deep.

2. Pour that water into the narrow jar.

3. Using a strip of masking tape to make a scale on the outside of the narrow jar (Figure 11). Mark the water level on the tape. Label that mark 1.0 inch.

4. Divide the inch into ten equal spaces (Figure 11).

5. Place the large jar in an open area away from buildings and trees. You might tape the jar to a stake or the top of a post.

6. Measure a rainfall by pouring water from the large jar into the smaller calibrated jar. Record the rainfall. If there is more than an inch, empty the first inch and continue to measure the additional amount. Be sure to check

WHAT YOU NEED:

- **water**
- **ruler**
- **large jar with straight vertical sides, such as a large peanut butter jar**
- **tall, narrow jar, such as an olive jar**
- **marking pen**
- **notebook**
- **pen or pencil**
- **masking tape**

Figure 11. You can make a rain gauge to measure rainfall.

the big jar every morning as it often rains at night.

7. Measure rainfall for at least one month. Record the rainfall each time it rains. At the end of the month, add your numbers to find the total rain for the month.

8. Grasslands receive 10 to 30 inches of rain per year. An average monthly rainfall would be between 0.8 and 2.5 inches. How does your rainfall compare with that of a grassland? Of course, a better comparison would be to record rainfall for more than one month.

What's Going On?

Depending on where you live, rainfall may be more or less than that found in a grassland.

Keep Exploring–If You Have More Time!

* An inch of snow contains less water than an inch of rain. Find a way to convert the depth of a snowfall to inches of rain. But remember, light fluffy snow contains less water per inch than wet slushy snow.

Words to Know

acre—An area of land equal to 43,560 square feet, 4,840 square yards, or 0.405 hectare.

aquifer—Permeable and porous rocks and soil containing large volumes of water. It is often the water source for cities, towns, farms, and ranches.

biome—A region of the earth with a characteristic climate and species of plants and animals.

climatogram—A graph that shows annual monthly rainfall and temperature for a particular place on earth, such as a city or town.

compacted soil—Soil that has been pressed together.

erosion—The wearing down, loosening, and movement of earth's surface by wind, water, gravity, and glaciers.

germination—The emergence of a baby plant from a seed.

global warming—The slowly increasing temperature of the earth caused by greenhouse gases.

greenhouse effect—The warming of earth's atmosphere by gases that trap solar energy like a greenhouse. These greenhouse gases absorb longwave (heat) radiation leaving the earth and reradiate it back to earth.

greenhouse gases—Gases such as carbon dioxide, methane, and nitrous oxide that trap longwave radiation (heat), causing global warming.

hectare—An area of land equal to 10,000 square meters, 100 ares, or 2.471 acres.

Homestead Act—An act passed by the United States Congress in 1862. It gave people 160 acres of western grassland if they were willing to settle there and farm the land.

Ogallala Aquifer—A huge aquifer that lies beneath a large portion of U.S. grassland.

wind turbine—A machine driven by wind that generates electricity.

Learn More

Books

Bardhan-Quallen, Sudipta. *Championship Science Fair Projects: 100 Sure-to-Win Experiments*. New York: Sterling, 2005.

Jackson, Kay. *Explore the Grasslands*. Mankato, Minn.: Capstone Press, 2007.

Latham, Donna. *Amazing Biome Projects You Can Build Yourself*. White River Junction, Vt.: Nomad Press, 2009.

Newland, Sonya. *Grassland Animals*. Mankato, Minn: Smart Apple Media, 2012.

Wallace, Marianne D. *America's Prairies and Grasslands*. Golden, Colo.: Fulcrum Publishing, 2008.

Web Sites

Biomes: Grasslands
<www.ducksters.com/science/ecosystems/grasslands_biome.php>

Grassland—Kids Do Ecology
<kids.nceas.ucsb.edu/biomes/grassland.html>

Index

A
acreage, calculating, 26–27
aquifers, 28–29, 38–41

B
bison, 5–6

C
climatograms, 14–15
cowboy hats, 24–25

D
desert biome, 42–43
drought, modeling, 38–41
Dust Bowl, 7, 36–37

E
electricity generation, 30–31
experiments, designing, 8–9

G
global warming, 32–35
grassland biomes, 4–7
Great Dust Storm, 19
greenhouse effect, 32–35

H
Homestead Act, 26–27
hypothesis, 8

M
map usage, 12–13
mercury, 10

N
notebooks, 11

O
Ogallala Aquifer, 28, 38, 41

P
pond biome, 43

R
rainfall gauge, 44–45
rain forest biome, 42–43

S
safety, 10–11
savannas, 5
science fairs, 9
scientific method, 8–9
seasons, 20–21
seed germination, 42–43
shade, 24–25
soil
  in aquifers, 28–29
  compacted, 16–17
  erosion, 18–19, 36–37
seed germination, 42–43
  temperature, shade and, 24–25

T
thermometers, 10
tundra biome, 42–43

V
variables, 8–9
volume, calculating, 28–29

W
water
  in aquifers, 28–29, 38–41
  evaporation, 22–23
  pollution, 40–41
  rainfall gauge, 44–45
wind
  evaporation, 22–23
  soil erosion, 18–19, 36–37
  turbine model, 30–31
winter sunlight, 20–21